# Cock Tales

# Cock Tales
## From Anonymity to the State House

## Mary F. Snelling

© 2016 Mary F. Snelling
Sir Big Spur ™. All rights reserved.

ISBN: 0692760237
ISBN 13: 9780692760239
Library of Congress Control Number: 2016912045
SirBigSpur, Aiken, SC

*Dedicated to those whose sacrificial love made the story of this book possible.*

**Figure 1:** Sir Big Spur's Roost in Aiken, South Carolina

# Table Of Contents

Foreword .................................................. xi

The Beginning ............................................. 1
Early Days ................................................ 2
Start of the Tradition .................................... 4
Lou ....................................................... 8
Cocky Too ................................................ 14
Mary ..................................................... 19
Roostergate .............................................. 20
Football Start ........................................... 22
Roost Roller I ........................................... 29
Caroline ................................................. 33
RV/Trailer ............................................... 37
Away Games: Georgia ...................................... 40
Away Games: Tennessee .................................... 42
Away Games: Others ....................................... 45
Baseball Again ........................................... 48
The Hawk ................................................. 52
Stephen Malkoff .......................................... 54
Roost Roller II .......................................... 57
"Most Involved Mascot in Sports" ......................... 60
Media Adventures ......................................... 62
Sir Big Spur Day ......................................... 66

Epilogue: Where Do We Go from Here ....................... 68
About the Author ......................................... 72
Contact Information ...................................... 73

# Foreword

This short book is part biography, part history, part comedy, part tragedy, part autobiography and completely full of a couple's love for each other and the University of South Carolina.

For over nineteen years, I, with my husband Ron, have bred, raised, carried and presented the live mascot for the university. This endeavor has been fun and rewarding from the perspective of meeting people and having unique experiences but personally costly in money and time. Other important life issues, such as church, family and friends, have been many times relegated to a place of lesser importance.

As of this date, June 15, 2016, I am rewriting the foreword of this book originally written in August of 2014. Now, as then, the final chapter is not done. Since 2014, Ron and I have tried, without success, to forge a partnership with the university that would allow us to recoup money spent and to make Sir Big Spur a lasting legacy for USC. The SBS brand, the gamecocks and all equipment have been bought and maintained by us at our expense. Most of the steps taken to make Sir Big Spur the recognizable representative of USC he is today were difficult and costly. We have fought like gamecocks but we are older now and have the usual challenges that come with age. We would be honored if our efforts with SBS were time well spent.

Failing to forge said partnership and considering the cost of time, money and effort necessary to perpetuate the SBS presence at and for USC, we decided to tell all publicly in hopes that a resolution can be reached.

Our plan is to honor the truth and trust God for the best outcome.

So here is the story of a labor of love.

Mary F. Snelling

Ron J. Albertelli

**Figure 2: Mary, her dad and Cocky-Doodle-Lou (SBS 1)**

# The Beginning

Hello. My name is Sir Big Spur. My human mom, Mary, calls me Spur when she is not mad at me or her number one rooster, Ron. I live in a used-to-be small town in the south of the United States where the winters are mild—not according to Mary—and the summers are hot enough to fry an egg on any smooth surface. By the way, this state is shaped like a piece of pie also made from eggs. (Funny how my whole world revolves around eggs and the humans.)

Well anyway, Mary was born to love THE major university in this small, hot pie-shaped state. She says she can't remember a time when she did not love that university, and when she got old enough, she spent six years there (BS in nursing and a Master's in public health). I didn't exist then in any form and my ancestors were blissfully unaware that this university existed. My ancestors were brought over from the motherland to entertain the gentry with a bloody, evil sport called cockfighting. Thankfully, this sport is illegal now!

Back to the story of me, Mary and Ron: Mary's sire worked at a plant where the cotton fabric from the mill was dyed. In fact, his title WAS dyer. He was an outgoing sort with many friends and one of those thought that his daughter ought to own the fowl that was her university's mascot. Now Dad loved that daughter and was excited to thrill her so he got a gamecock from that friend and presented that rooster to Mary. She was happy that her dad loved her that much but she had no clue what to do with that cock.

And so the story begins…

## Early Days

Mary and Ron allowed my great-granddaddy (Lou) to roam the farm. He roosted in trees and left love offerings on the porches but, much like Adam in the book of Genesis in the Bible, he was lonely. So Mary went back to the source of my great-granddaddy and got some hens to keep him company. Now this small flock thrived, made eggs, slept in trees and multiplied. That got kind of out of hand—you know, like orange-dressed people on a Saturday in the fall. So Mary and Ron built them some homes not affectionately called cages and their roaming days were soon to be over. But Ron, being a Yankee-born city slicker, did not know how to catch the flock and the fun began. He tried to entice the flock to go into inverted boxes with strings that he could pull to drop the boxes on top of the gamecocks. Sorry, I was not there but Mary still doubles over in laughter when she tells how the gamecocks were smarter and faster than Ron. (You have to hear the one about how he tried to capture a newborn calf separated from her mom with a tractor and a motor home.) After several days of these inventive but ineffective methods to catch the original flock, Ron discovered that they roosted in trees after dark and slept so soundly that he could just walk up and pluck (bad word) them off the branches. Thus ended freedom and free-range chickens in the Sanctuary.

**Figure 3: Mary, Ron and Cocky-Doodle-Lou (SBS 1) early days**

## Start of the Tradition

Well, you ask, how did you go from being a caged pet on a horse farm to a highly recognizable, much televised, live mascot of a major university? Good question. In fact, a much better question than the ones Mary and Ron get asked regularly but we'll get to that later…

Mary LOVES Gamecock sports and back in the day of my great-granddaddy, USC baseball was not what it is today. The dirt roosters (baseball team) played in the cozy confines of Sarge Frye Field, season tickets were sold on a punch card and the purchaser could choose which of the games to attend and have the card punched. Seating was not assigned. In fact, Mary and Mr. OOT-OOT (Bill Golding) used to save their seats with seat cushions. Mary never does anything halfheartedly so she sat by B-Rob's (Brian Roberts') dad for a year and learned the finer arts of college baseball, like how to play pickle and pitcher hints to steal bases. Also, Mrs. Sudie (Love) with her wonderful chicken hats taught Mary how to score and now Mary has many, many full score books. Ron says that scoring keeps Mary less nervous and therefore less likely to get upset with him and me when things don't go well in the dirt so big thanks to Mrs. Sudie.

**Figure 4: Mr. OOT-OOT (Bill Golding) and Cocky-Doodle-Lou (SBS 1)**

Figure 5: Mrs. Sudie Love, Cocky-Doodle-Lou (SBS 1) and one of her wonderful hats

So one game Mary was scoring and the public address announcer talked about how to win a free dinner with the new coach, Ray Tanner. Mary entered and won and was she excited.

This fabulous dinner was at a local BBQ house. Mary HATES BBQ but at least it wasn't at Kentucky Fried…hate to eat my distant kin, you know. At this dinner, Mary and Ron told Coach about my great-granddaddy and asked him if they could bring the cock to the baseball games and put him on top of the dugout. Coach said as long as it wasn't between the white lines, he didn't mind but if it got to be a problem, he would let them know. So Mary and Ron hurried to give the cock a name and a persona. Lou Holtz was the football coach at the time and Cocky-Doodle-Lou just had a ring to it so that became my great-granddaddy's name and the fun began.

## Lou

My great-granddaddy said that those first years were frightening, entertaining and a huge learning curve (and not just for him). He thought the hawks nesting in the light poles at Sarge Frye were just waiting on dinner every game. It seemed like the dirt rooster with the bat in hand was aiming foul balls at him but it was fun when those novice dirt roosters came out of the dugout with an expression of amazement and disbelief, pointed at him and said, "What's that?" Even some of the southern-born boys didn't know what a real, live black-breasted red Old English Gamecock looked like. And the fans…some of the most ridiculous questions you could imagine! For example, is the rooster a boy or a girl? Does the rooster lay eggs? Quickly Ron and Mary realized one of their new tasks was to educate the Gamecock faithful about gamecocks. Now, Ron is one of the most patient people God ever created but Mary…that's another story. She loved to talk with the children and her favorite all-time question came from an eleven-year-boy about whether gamecocks pass gas. (Her answer was she didn't know but would pay closer attention.) However, Mary quickly grew tired of the adults asking those questions so that became one of patient Ron's many tasks in this still-new experience.

**Figure 6: Coach Lou Holtz and Mary with Cocky-Doodle-Lou (SBS 1)**

**Figure 7: Cocky-Doodle-Lou (SBS 1) on dugout at Sarge Frye Field**

**Figure 8: Ron answering questions at Sarge Frye Field**

Things went along this way for a while. The dirt roosters got better; Mary and Ron answered questions, made lots of friends and just generally loved Gamecock baseball. Coach Tanner had that same competitive, intense demeanor as Mary and in 2000 the team was special. They all thought they were going to Omaha, the home of the College World Series. Coach Tanner and Mary had never been but wanted to go something terrible. Having never traveled much, Great-Granddaddy Lou thought it sounded awful to ride all that way and leave his number two girl, Louella, home but for Mary (number one but who's counting?), Omaha was Mecca and Lou was willing to do his part. Well, on a REALLY hot day in Columbia, some bleach-headed boys from Louisiana burst Mary's and Coach's bubbles. Since those Cajun boys had been talking about gumbo and Granddaddy Lou in the same sentence, he was relieved to be going home to Aiken. It took another couple of years for the dirt roosters to have a chance to go to Omaha. Lou told about a home run against Miami and how Mary burst into tears she was so happy. Mary had trouble getting away from work to drive those twenty-two hours to Omaha and they got there just as the first game against Georgia Tech was starting. Mary says when she and Ron drove up, there was a line of Nebraska Huskies wrapped around the stadium and she thought she was not going to be able to get into Rosenblatt but she did. Those dirt roosters got whipped, 11–0. Mary thought, "We are not going to drive all this way and lose two games and go home. No way!" So she and Ron cooked up this plan…

Figure 9: **Cocky-Doodle-Lou (SBS 1) in front of Rosenblatt Stadium, Omaha**

Figure 10: Cocky-Doodle-Lou (SBS 1) on pitcher's mound, Rosenblatt Stadium, Omaha

They found the stadium superintendent for Rosenblatt and told him they needed to take some promotional pictures of Lou on the field. Mr. Jesse Cuevas thought that odd but went along. There are some great pictures of Great-Granddaddy on the pitcher's mound but more importantly, he left a small deposit on that mound and just flat-out killed the chicken curse. The dirt roosters went all the way to the final game and, had the format been like it is today (final series of best of three), they would probably have won it. Houston Street and the Longhorns were just too good but what a ride.

Now neither Great-Granddaddy Lou nor any of the rest of us has actually gotten inside Rosenblatt for a game. That would be against the NCAA rules about mascots but Mary and Ron devised another plan to represent us and to get USC some national recognition. Enter Cocky Too…

# Cocky Too

Cocky Too, our traveling companion and alter ego…

That NCAA rule against live mascots just kept cropping up and hindering Mary and Ron. Plus finally, after years and many dollars, the VW (that's Caroline and another story) was ready to roll. If any of us real Gamecocks sit in the back seat, we can't be seen AND as Mary says (too often) we are not house or car trained—if you get my meaning. I guess it's OK on a pitcher's mound in Omaha but not too cool in the backseat.

Mary is not the big shopper that many other women are but as I always say, she IS persistent. Addams Book Store, when it was on the corner of Main and Blossom, had a store display of a six-foot stuffed animal that looked like our human mascot, Cocky. This doll stood proud and tall until the little humans kept crawling on him and punching him. Then he sat in a corner and still enthralled the public. Well, Mary thought this doll would be PERFECT in the back seat of the VW and proceeded to try to buy him. Great-Granddaddy says he lost track of how many times Mary went into that store and tried to buy him. The store manager told Mary, "It is not for sale." That manager did not know Mary. She can worry warts off frogs when she sets her mind and set it she did. Finally, one day, the exasperated store manager stated a price he figured any sane human would find laughable. Mary said, "SOLD," and she and her friend Kay stuffed him in the trunk of a Honda and went on back to the football tailgating party. Now, Mary thought, "What a perfect Christmas gift for Ron." So she sneaked the doll home. She and her mom and dad found a refrigerator box and spent a day wrapping it in Christmas paper and hiding it.

Mary could hardly wait to give it to Ron.

**Figure 11: Ron and Cocky Too on Christmas**

He was surprised and pleased.

That is until he had to start carrying the hundred-plus-pound doll into Hoover (SEC Baseball Tournament location) and Omaha. They named the doll Cocky Too and paid the full ticket price for him to attend all the games USC played in the College World Series at Rosenblatt. Cocky Too has his own baseball cap, which was a car topper for a national auto-parts store. He also has his own football helmet, which started life as a charcoal grill. He's also wired to crow (and sound like me). You have to give it to Mary and Ron for creativity and dedication.

And the three became four with more to come…

**Figure 12: The crew in Rosenblatt, Omaha**

# Mary

As I said early on, Gamecock life did not start for Mary with me and my ancestors. She watched George run, bought all-black clothes in 1984, ranted and raved when Mop Head Cremins went all the way to the altar and got cold feet, loved Grayson Greiner's dad and his Irish coach and just generally enjoyed all things Gamecock. She sat through every minute of the football team going 0–21, even one bitterly cold night when Florida stomped USC and there were only six people left in the upper deck at Willy B (nickname for the football stadium). She was there when the goalposts came down and just could not figure out how to get to the field or she might have made that walk to five points. She does not like the Gamecocks of any sport to display classlessness (too much like the rednecks from the west) so she walked out early from two games with the orange-clad neighbors to the north in protest of OUR behavior.

We are not talking fair-weather fan or in it just to show off me and my ancestors. We are talking serious love. Mary's dad used to say he hoped he didn't die on the day of a Gamecock game because Mary might not be available for his funeral. (He didn't and she was.)

So the next two stories are the low and the high for Mary and her love for all things Gamecock.

# Roostergate

Mary's grandmother used to say to take the medicine before the sugar so for the worst story of our history (at least for now—the final chapter of this story is yet to happen)...

In 2004, baseball was going along as usual. The dirt roosters were good, attendance was great, Ron was answering questions, Lou was strutting on top of the first base dugout and Mary was keeping score and talking with Kay, Darrell, Edith, Imogene, Ashton and Jake. Kay and Mary were into the early-season voting on the cutest butt on the team. (Brian Buscher has the all-time award in this category.) The seats to the right of Mary were empty at the start of the game when two women never seen before or since arrived. The younger one called the owner of the seats, who had also never been there, and said, "These seats are great. We are so close we can smell the rooster." And so began Roostergate.

It turns out the absentee seat holder was a big-time booster who owned some restaurants in town. He wanted to throw some weight around, not realizing he was just a bantam, so he called the university and stirred the proverbial hornet's nest by demanding that Lou be banned. Now by this time, Granddaddy Lou had been on that dugout for five years. He had been petted by many children, their parents and grandparents had talked to Ron and Mary, the dirt roosters loved it when he crowed, he had killed the chicken curse at Omaha and he was a fan favorite. The university was caught between a rock and a hard place. They banned Lou. Media from around town, around the state and around the nation got involved in the ruckus between a university and its mascot. Leonard's Losers picked USC, *Sports Illustrated* had Lou's picture, newspapers from Seattle and California had articles, ESPN called Mary at WORK and generally it was a cockfight. Mary and Ron were amazed, upset and disappointed so they decided to try the case in the court of public opinion. Ron had thousands of "Cocky-Doodle-Lou, We love you stickers" in fluorescent yellow made and Mary, with the help of Jake, circulated petitions.

The fans did cheers like "In with the rooster, out with the booster" and were tremendously supportive. Ron and Mary were interviewed by many media outlets and their story then, as it is now, was "We love the university and are just trying to do our part to make it special." Roostergate blew over when Mr. Mike McGee, athletics director, after returning from SEC Media Days, looked up from Sarge's field and said to Mary, "Ms. Snelling, your gamecock is welcome here any time." You know that big booster did not fare well for picking a fight with a university mascot in a university town. And Lou went on to more fame and learned football…

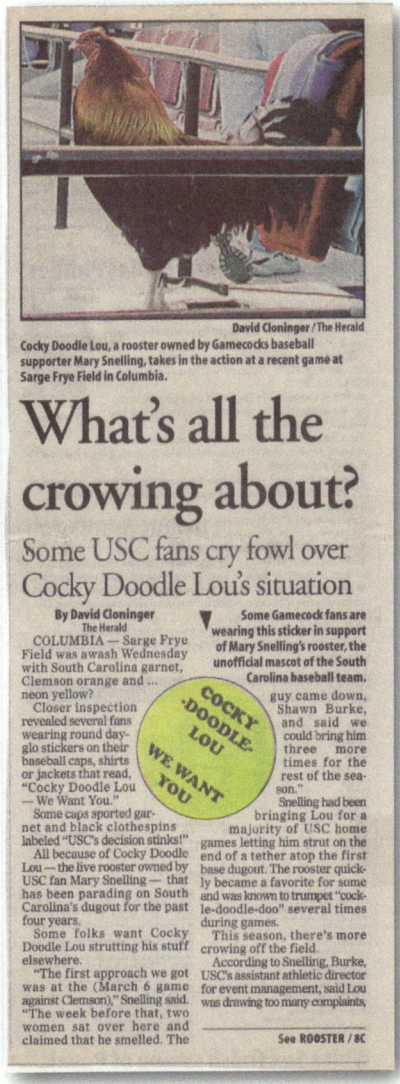

Figure 13: Local newspaper carries story of Roostergate.
Used by permission of David Cloninger

# Football Start

In 2006, a year after he became athletics director at USC, Eric Hyman formed a focus group of diverse people who loved the school to suggest ideas to improve the game-day experience at Willy B. One of their many ideas was to invite the people who brought the gamecock to baseball to bring him to football. So Mary was called and asked. About as quickly and enthusiastically as I greet the first hint of dawn each day, she said a resounding YES. I mean, does it get any better for a Gamecock-loving human than to get to merge the love for my great-granddaddy, the university and football?

The first order of business was to give Great-Granddaddy Lou a new name. It just was not fitting to have him named after a coach who was no longer there and the thought was to give him a name that would transcend current people and events. Mary and Ron brainstormed, debated and tried out many names. Finally, Mary thought of the original Cocky, Big Spur. Big Spur was extremely ugly and scared children so he was retired before 1980. Ron thought that adding Sir before Big Spur would give us our own unique identity but tie us to USC tradition and thus Cocky-Doodle-Lou became Sir Big Spur (SBS) I. Lou was getting up in years but deserved to make the circuit that first football year.

RIGHT: Imposing Big Spur was the predecessor to Cocky.

**Figure 14: Sir Big Spur's namesake**

**Figure 15: Cocky and SBS**

Then, one day, Mary came home from a long day of nursing and erected in the garden was a full-size goalpost. Just not what you think you'd see in your yard. Ron was out there with Great-Granddaddy trying to teach him to sit on the goalpost and not fly off. SBS I learned this necessary skill the same way SBS II and III and I have learned it: by trial and error. The error is when we are tethered to the goalpost and fly off; we don't go very far and seeing the world upside down is just plain not pleasant. We may not be the smartest creature God created but we learn some things very fast. Mary and Ron have been asked many times if we can be taught to crow on demand; we aren't that smart either (but then neither is the person asking the question).

**Figure 16: SBS training ground**

Mary and Ron had no idea what game day would involve but they thought they were ready. On September 9, 2006, they rolled Sir Big Spur I down Assembly Street to George Rogers Boulevard in a dog cage on a luggage carrier. Ron had built a goalpost out of PVC pipe, which he carried (reminded Mary of another man carrying a cross up a hill outside Jerusalem). They dodged traffic and SBS I suffered the bumps of the road. When they got to the stadium, there was no way to make the goalpost stay upright. The next week, Ron carried the goalposts and fifty pounds of weight down the same path. The third game, Ron and Mary convinced USC to allow them to leave the goalposts and the weights at the stadium. Thankfully, they did not leave SBS I but took him home to my great-grandmamma. That season was filled with learning experiences for everyone but was thrilling to Mary. She tells about how big the football players are up close and personal and how you can't see anything from the sidelines except the cheerleaders (remember Mary loves sports, not pageantry, no matter how good). An EMT took pity on Ron and Mary and gave them some earplugs because those speakers down by the flagpole are LOUD. Mary could not see the plays develop as she could in her seats in the upper deck and did not get to enjoy the subtleties of the game but she nearly expired from excitement when the 2001 entrance was done and she was on the field. All in all it was a great experience for SBS I and his crew. The fans, especially the students, were supportive and the university asked them to do it again the next year. However, Ron, with his engineering, problem-solving mind, decided that some new means of moving SBS and his stuff to the field from the parking lot needed to be devised. And so the Roost Roller was developed completely from Ron's imagination and at much expense of time and money.

# Roost Roller I

**Figure 17: The Roost Roller I and driver**

Ron first bought a toy from Walmart—a green gator made for children to ride. After stripping it down, he proceeded to devise a plan to make it remote controlled. Now, Ron has a lot of talents in building most anything and figuring out how things work but he knew NOTHING about servos and remote controls and so on. So he called people in California and talked with the manager of the local hobby shop and he spent lots of money. In fact, Mary thought a nice, long cruise would certainly have been a better utilization of that money but Ron persevered. When he got the "thing" to roll around by remote control the first time, he was like an overgrown boy with an oversized toy. He designed it to hold the goalpost and with a shelf to hold the cage with SBS in it until game time. He painted it black and gave it lights. The other details were added gradually as thoughts occurred: Mary won the Cocky driver shooting basketballs at the state fair that year, the rooster horn was confiscated from other uses and added, the ability to fly a Gamecock flag was also added to draw attention and let the crowd know when SBS arrived and so on.

Figure 18: The Roost Roller I on Williams-Brice Field

And so, starting with year 2 of football, SBS came down Assembly Street to George Rogers to Willy B (a route familiar to all serious Gamecock football fans) on the Roost Roller. Talk about dodging traffic. The next problem was the Roost Roller would run out of battery power before getting back to the parking lot and there was a lot of pushing done by some tired, hot humans. So Ron added more batteries and more weight. It continued to be a labor of love; some days it seemed the labor outweighed the love.

Ron and Mary asked the university for parking at the stadium. As any long-time Carolina football attendee knows, parking around the stadium was like the Promised Land: given by God and inherited. So Ron and Mary were given a parking space on Key Road. This space did not allow the RV to be parked. A way to get the Roost Roller to the parking space had to be devised. Ron built the Roost Roller Transport, a trailer just the right size to hold the Roost Roller. Then one asks, how does the trailer with the roller inside get to the Key Road lot and then to the stadium? Good question. Enter Caroline…

# Caroline

One night many years ago, Ron and Mary were traveling to Columbia from Aiken, a trip that has been made many, many times. As they turned from Highway 378 onto Gervais Street, at a gas station that no longer exists sat this old, tired, rusted-out VW convertible. They started talking about how that would be the perfect car to pull behind the RV on their many Gamecock-focused travels. So Ron negotiated a price and dragged that old thing home. Now, Mary and Ron's son-in-law is of German descent and he loves VWs. He was asked to restore the VW. After about ten years and many thousands of dollars spent on genuine replacement parts and paint, Caroline was born. She is a 1979 VW convertible. This was the last year they were made in the United States before the tooling was sent Mexico.

Ron and Mary fitted her up with some embroidered seat covers (done by the same friend who does the SBS Crew clothing, Mr. Jim Hanna). With a little help, Cocky Too fits in the back seat. Caroline has her own speaker system that plays all the popular Gamecock music and a travel hitch to pull the Roost Roller Transport. Mary gave Caroline some beauty and personality with the addition of eyelashes.

When Caroline is pulling the Roost Roller Transport with the Roost Roller on the tailgate and Cocky Too in the back seat, the sight is a Gamecock fantasy. I (or my sires) ride on top of the Roost Roller when we are in parades. Otherwise, I ride inside the Roost Roller Transport.

**Figure 19: Parade and football ready**

Speaking of parades, one of the most delightful and scary nights ever happened with all of us at a parade in Ybor City (Tampa, Florida) before an Outback Bowl. Seems like someone in the Athletics Department at USC does not have the attention to detail Mary has and this person forgot to arrange a ride for the university president, Dr. Harris Pastides, and his hen, Mrs. Patricia-Moore Pastides. So Mary and Ron offered them a ride in Caroline with the rest of us. We gave them some beads to throw and it was FUN. Although they weren't born as southerners or Gamecocks, "They got here as quick as they could," as Mary's mother used to say, and they certainly exhibit all the wonderful characteristics of true southerners: grace, manners and open hearts. Well, things were going along beautifully until the end of the parade, when we had to get them back to the start of the parade route to meet their ride. They were sitting on the back of Caroline and Ron took a wrong turn. We were traveling through some rather seedy areas of Tampa when Dr. Pastides stated he hoped he did not make the home newspaper because he was shot. Mary got a headache and missed the remainder of the New Year's Eve festivities but we got them safely to the rendezvous point—whew!

Figure 20: The president and first lady with Caroline and her lashes in Tampa. Picture courtesy of CJDriggers @GamecockCentral.com

# RV/Trailer

As you might imagine, getting all this equipment to Columbia from the home farm in Aiken became quite a production. With all the additional traveling that started when the baseball team became more successful back in the early 2000s, they bought a new RV. It was the wrong color and was just generally bland but Ron liked the engine (of all things) and the manufacturer so it became the new mode of transportation. Since then, of course, it has been painted the right colors and it has a big, bold, beautiful mural of Great-Granddaddy Lou on the back (as Sir Big Spur of course). Mary had the Gamecock carpet installed as a birthday present for Ron and now this machine is just Gamecock all the way.

With the addition of Caroline and Cocky Too and the Roost Roller and the Roost Roller Transport, some means of getting down the road had to be devised. So a twenty-four-foot trailer that is pulled behind the RV was added. It is equipped with special tie-downs because Ron isn't the smoothest driver in the world—that's what Mary says anyway. I really don't have any experience with any other drivers especially since Mary refuses to drive the rig. Anyway, going down the road, we are longer than an eighteen-wheeler and unmistakably Gamecocks. Although to travel like this is necessary to transport all of us (no hotels take chickens), it sure limits where we can go. Most restaurants don't have parking, we don't park in the Key Road lot or the stadium and in general our travels require some coordination and advanced planning. Ron is famous around the RV community for his skill in maintaining, repairing and most of all backing up this conglomeration. We are also popular at the Walmart stores around Columbia, especially the one in Lexington, where we have resided on football weekends.

Figure 21: RV with mural of SBS

After the first College World Series adventure, when we were parked next to a Bluebird bus that could play music, Mary ordered a sound system for the roof that will blow your ears off. It plays "Step to the Rear," "2001," "Take Me Out to the Ballgame," "The Chicken Dance," "Taps" and so on. One time some UGA fans parked behind the RV just kept barking and disturbing Mary. I mean, what adult human barks? So every time they barked, she played the fight song. They initiated a truce. They would quit if she would. Gamecocks 1, Bulldogs 0.

**Figure 22: All decked out—notice the horns**

# Away Games: Georgia

So back to football...

In 2007, Mary and Ron asked if they could go and be on the sidelines at the sites of away football games. They had seen UGA (Mary calls him UGLY) and Smokey (University of Tennessee's live mascot) at Willy B and thought this would be fun and would let some more of the college sport world see the spirit and beauty of a real Fighting Gamecock.

Our first adventure outside the friendly confines of Willy B was Sanford Stadium, home of the University of Georgia Bulldogs. The maddest Mary has ever been at a college sporting event was at the Georgia's baseball stadium when an inebriated adult "fan" made a disgusting remark about her mother. It was good that day that Mary realized she was a bantam and that words are more powerful than the sword. But it was with trepidation that the crew traveled to Athens. Their concern was misplaced. The experience was well choreographed by the UGA Athletic Department. We were given parking close to the stadium without difficult egress and the fans, although not fond of our gridiron boys or us, were civil and orderly. Mary was excited to be "between the hedges" especially since she had worked for many years in the state of Georgia and had endured endless taunts. Whether we won or not, she was the envy of many of her coworkers because of those hallowed hedges (overrated if you ask my opinion). And that Bulldog? What a waste. Too overweight to move and needs to sit on ice just to survive the game—where's his fighting spirit? SBS and crew have been on the field at UGA four times now—we missed 2009 due to a failure in communication. The second time SBS III got to meet the governor of South Carolina (*she's a Clemson fan?*) and we marched in with USC's band, which was thrilling until we got to the huge stairs, which were a problem for Mary and Ron since my transportation does not do stairs. So SBS and Mary and Ron and the Roost Roller had to find their way through the red-and-black-clad fans to the only elevator in Sanford Stadium. A little scary and would have been really scary in the reverse after the game had we lost but we did NOT, thanks in large part to Melvin Ingram. Dr. and Mrs. Pastides came down to the field toward the end of the game and there were high fives all around. That year was my first time at Georgia and boy, was it hot but fun. Mary got a little upset with a university official who asked, "How is he/she doing?" Now don't disparage my manhood—I am a cock, I don't lay eggs and I crow when I feel like it. One would think a person in his position would know that…

**Figure 23: SBS eating between the hedges**

# Away Games: Tennessee

Next on our travels was Neyland Stadium, home of the Tennessee Volunteers. Of all the places we have traveled to as the live mascot for USC, Tennessee does the best job of coordinating and protecting the opposing team's mascot. We are given excellent parking that is directed and protected, the SBS crew is given its own motorcycle patrolmen to get us through the crowd and onto the field, and after the game, these guys come back in and get us through the crowd to our transport and into traffic. Ron always feels like the president and Mary, the feisty one, is protected from any deleterious effects of her verbal opinions. Sometimes I think she should have been the fighting one of the crew but that's another tangent.

The first year, 2007, the crew was underneath Neyland waiting on the football team to arrive. Ron was having a conversation with a fan about the finer aspects of raising gamecocks. A distraught woman and her sister approached Mary. The woman was dressed in garnet and black and was in tears. She quickly told the story of the recent death of her husband, who was a Tennessee fan, and how he had asked to have his ashes spread on both Willy B's and Neyland's fields. She pulled a baggie out of her purse with the ashes and asked Mary if she would take the ashes in and spread them. That is the only time a SBS has seen Mary speechless. Mary motioned for Ron but by the time he came over, the woman had spread the ashes on the Roost Roller. Now, we always used to wear black when we played Tennessee because it is usually Halloween weekend and orange and black…you know. Well, all through that game, Mary kept getting ashes on her black outfit. Since that day, Mary lost her parents so her empathy for that woman is greater now that it was that night. That night the crew was flabbergasted and the next morning all was washed.

**Figure 24: SBS at Neyland Stadium—SPOOKY!**

# Away Games: Others

The crew has also been on the away fields of Auburn, Alabama, LSU, Ole Miss, Mississippi State, Florida, Missouri, Kentucky, UCF, the SEC Championship and six bowl games. Arkansas and Vanderbilt do not allow live mascots—what does that make the hog? We all hope to be on the field at Texas A&M in the future. (This happened in 2015 and was an unforgettable experience.)

Auburn was wonderful. We had great parking and were absolutely treated with respect. The Auburn fans are the most welcoming and helpful of all we have encountered. Mary states the first time she was there, she was completely overwhelmed by the number of times she was "welcomed to Auburn." From my perspective, Auburn was a bit unusual. I had to stay inside my coop until the end of the first quarter because the War Eagle grandly flies down and around the stadium to the center of the field in the pregame festivities and then is walked around the stadium during the first quarter to meet and greet his many fans. The reason he is so amenable to this show is that he is fed meat when he arrives at midfield. Mary, Ron and Mr. Crow, the previous, very congenial manager of the War Eagle, thought it would be bad form if I became the meat. So I was kept enclosed and I am THANKFUL!

**Figure 25: SBS and Auburn War Eagle**

A funny thing happened at Florida. As we went onto the field with the Roost Roller, Mary and Ron were hurriedly approached by a Florida official who informed them that no motorized carts were allowed on the field. When he was informed the cart was battery operated, he asked for a second opinion and still the cart was not allowed on the field. Ron offered to take the batteries out and roll it on the field—still no go. So the cart was left outside unprotected and vulnerable and Ron and Mary carried me and the goalpost inside. The only means available to erect the goalpost was to stick it in a drainage vent and bungee-cord it in place. The post was not very stable, we were close to the foul (not fowl)–mouthed Florida student section, it rained like crazy, the magnets were stolen off of Caroline and we lost. Other than that it was a wonderful night…

Figure 26: On Gator Field without the Roost Roller

All the other sites, with the exception of Kentucky, have been fun and safe. Kentucky had never beaten Steve Spurrier and the night it happened, the Wildcats became truly wild. They jumped over the wall and over our heads as they headed to the field to celebrate. There was little crowd control. Finally, we were placed under the stadium and behind a chain link fence until the crowd calmed and dissipated. Then two bicycle patrolmen escorted us to Caroline, waited for us to load and then rode with us to the entrance of the parking lot. Ron always says this is the only time he has felt threatened during our many adventures. By the way, the next time we were in Kentucky, we won and there were no problems.

# Baseball Again

Let's take a diversion back to baseball for a minute.

Baseball is Mary's favorite sport. She loves the familial atmosphere, the class and intelligence of the dirt roosters, the weekend series, the weather going from winter to summer and the complexity of scoring the game. She also loved Sarge Frye Field. So when we started moving to the new stadium, Mary was excited but sad. Then she got mad when she could not get the seats on top of the first base dugout and I could not strut on same. No amount of discussion, case pleading or rational thinking could persuade the athletics administration to let us retain our favorite seats. Finally, after weeks of discussion, the true reason was admitted and a compromise was reached. Ron was pleased because we are now on the concourse and I can be better accessed by fans and Ron can interact with the Gamecock faithful, especially the biddies.

Figure 27: SBS Corner at baseball

Mary has grown to love our spot as well especially since it has now been dubbed "Sir Big Spur Corner" but she still complains she does not sit near our circle of friends from the Sarge and she is not close enough to rate the dirt roosters' butts. So that yearly contest is no longer.

When we won that first national championship at Rosenblatt, my granddaddy was there—outside the stadium but there. Cocky Too was inside with Mary and Ron. Granddaddy said he had seen Mary happy before but not like that. She kept saying, "I did live long enough." Then we did it again the next year in the new stadium. I told you Great-Granddaddy Lou killed the chicken curse in Omaha…

**Figure 28: SBS at Omaha**

**Figure 29: SBS immediately after the first national championship**

# The Hawk

There was another threatening time to the SBS line that could have ended the entire endeavor without the quick thinking and bravery of Ron…

Mary went to a nursing conference at the convention center and Ron and SBS III stayed outside by the RV. It was a cold winter day—early baseball season. Ron was inside the RV and Daddy was outside tethered to his coop. Ron looked out and a hawk had swooped down, believing he had found his dinner. Ron was barefoot and scantily dressed but he ran out the door. He thought that would scare the hawk away but that hawk was hungry…Ron attempted to shoo him away to no avail. As SBS III was tethered, an unfair fight was happening and SBS was losing. So Ron did what all of you would have done: he grabbed the hawk. The hawk was not aggressive to Ron but had some large nasty talons and a big hooked beak. Can you imagine barefoot, cold Ron standing out there alone, holding a hawk? He was not sure what to do so he stuffed the hawk into a collapsible trash can and zipped the lid. Then he took SBS into the RV to soothe ruffled feathers and calm them both down. About that time, Mary gets out of the conference, walks to the RV, sees the cage and no SBS, sees the trash can hopping in the parking lot and thinks Ron has lost his mind to put SBS in the trash can. She was surprised to hear the real story and then she took some amazing pictures of the hawk. Mary, being the feisty one, wanted to do bodily harm to that hawk for daring to think of SBS as dinner but cooler heads prevailed and the hawk was released. He flew to the top of Colonial Life Arena and watched for another opportunity to get dinner. Of course, he was not given that opportunity. That weekend some coeds told Mary and Ron that the hawk was familiar around campus and usually was seen with a small companion bird.

**Figure 30: Second most beautiful bird**

# Stephen Malkoff

Stephen Malkoff, an artist renowned for his renderings of famous trees (such as the Angel Oak on John's Island, South Carolina), called Mary one day and told her he would like to draw me. He had started a series on the live mascots of some of the universities in the south and had already done Auburn, Alabama and Clemson. Mary quickly researched his work, talked with Ron and became excited about Mr. Malkoff's interest in me. Mary and Stephen were simpatico on their Christian beliefs and immediately felt like close friends. One really hot day, Mr. Malkoff drove to Aiken and spent hours photographing me in multiple locations and lighting situations. It was BORING but Mary and Ron were happy so I posed. Months went by. When Mr. Malkoff had a particularly successful day drawing some facet of me, he and Mary would have a long telephone conversation. The most amazing thing about this process is that Mr. Malkoff uses ONLY a number 2 pencil so the details are tedious to get perfect. He has what Mary and Mrs. Malkoff call an artistic temperament, which means his work has to be perfect to him and when it is not, duck—like when foul balls head to Sir Big Spur's Corner in baseball or a fade pattern comes into our end zone in football. Finally, it was done. Mr. Malkoff acted like Louetta when the biddies hatch in the spring—sort of cocky. After the printing and framing, Mr. Malkoff became a regular in South Carolina (he lives in Alabama and is a big War Eagle fan). He peddled my picture everywhere. The *Spurs and Feathers* featured an article about the portrait and Mr. Malkoff. Some businesses sold the prints and Mary and Ron displayed a copy during football season that year. Sales were poor, which is a shame because I am the handsomest cock in the world and very proud to represent USC. Probably would have helped sales if our alma mater could have managed to support the process but that is part of a later story…

 Print #1 hangs in Mary and Ron's house, #3 hangs in Mary's brother's office and #2 was presented by Mary and Ron to Dr. Pastides, who stated he would find a prominent place to hang it. The other low-number prints are framed and ready for other USC coaches and venues.

**Figure 31: Dr. Pastides, Ron and Mary with Malkoff print**

# Roost Roller II

After eight years of heavy use, it was time for me to have a new ride. The Roost Roller I had seen some fun times at Willy B, Carolina Stadium, Omaha, parades, away venues, charity functions and so on and she was showing her age. So Ron and Mary cooked up an idea to build a new one with the help of USC's College of Nursing (Mary's school) and USC's College of Engineering and Computing. They met with Dean Andrews from the CON, who graciously agreed to help fund the new ride, and then they met with Professor Roger Dougal from engineering, who agreed that the design and prototype for the new ride could be a project for senior engineering students. The CON students raised money by selling Christmas ornaments. The engineering students were excited to have a project of interest to them. Both schools' students were very engaged and engaging on this project. As has been the case since the inception of the Sir Big Spur idea, there were unforeseen difficulties. For example, how does money flow from one school to another? It WAS possible and after months of waiting, the prototype for the Roost Roller II was done. With the help of Mary's friend Kathryn, we issued a press release and invited the Colleges of Nursing and of Engineering and Computing, the local media and USC administrators to attend the debut of Roost Roller II on a Friday afternoon before the first football game in the shadows of Willy B. All who were invited were represented except USC administrators.

**Figure 32: And this is better than Tahiti?**

Well, anyhow, the Roost Roller II is a one-of-a-kind remote-controlled transport with lights, music and maneuverability that displays me in style and lets me get in and out of all venues. I feel like the cock of the walk (or ride) for sure and the human biddies always want to drive it or have one of their own. I get photographed and filmed in it a lot but then I have been getting videoed and photographed a lot for a long time…

**Figure 33:** Roost Roller II in front of George Rogers' statue

# "Most Involved Mascot in Sports"

Ron came up with this moniker and promptly had a sign stating this placed over my head on the roost. He also had T-shirts and car magnets made with the statement.

This logo has engendered hundreds of questions from Carolina fans, other sports fans, the media and so on (which is exactly what Ron intended). You see, Mary, Ron and I go to anything the university invites us to or allows us to go to. We have been to soccer games, softball games, equestrian events and golf matches and would go to basketball if I were house trained—whatever that means. We also go to places outside of sports. We have gone to nursing homes, schools, charity events, parades, birthday parties, preseason parties, tailgate parties, MD offices and so on. Personally, some of them are fun and others just tiring. BUT Mary and Ron are committed to the advancement of the good name of the University of South Carolina and think of me and my traveling equipment as a way to not only polish that name but spread goodwill to others. So we go.

Occasionally, Mary and Ron get free food or small gifts for their efforts but usually it is just another expense of time and money on their parts to do their part. I get loved by the people and especially by my main squeezes, Ron and Mary (sometimes I get special food like bugs and nachos too!)

Hey, top that, UGA or Smokey.

**Figure 34: MOST involved mascot**

# Media Adventures

I've told you about Roostergate and all the media interest that engendered. However, that was just the top of the water dish compared to what has happened since then.

After we got invited to start being on the sideline at Willy B, Bob Gillespie interviewed us and wrote an article for the inaugural edition of *GO Gamecocks*, the magazine. We had a hard time not letting it go to our heads. Then many more opportunities for fame came. Mary's favorite was being interviewed for the *Carolinian* (the alumni magazine) and getting her picture taken with me on the Horseshoe. There was some story about a ball rotating on a statue that caused Mary to have a good laugh?! Ron's most memorable was flying home from Montana during vacation to meet ESPN at home to spend four hours in the August sun taking ONE picture for the magazine's article on live mascots of the SEC. It is a great picture, if I say so myself. Ron then flew back to Montana to get Mary.

My favorite media experience was drinking wine with Kirk Herbstreit and Lee Corso on the *GameDay* stage. Ron sneaking me up from behind the stage and Kirk Herbstreit being scared of me was a hoot (or is that a crow?). The story is that Mr. Corso had been building up my ferociousness and overstating my lack of control all morning so Mr. Herbstreit did not know what to expect.

Of course, one of my other favorite media memories was posing for the Gamecock Club Calendar in 2010. I was the March stud but it was not an R-rated (as in naked) calendar.

I have been in a cookbook, in the *State*, the *Aiken Standard* and multiple other newspapers, on ESPN innumerable times, listed in top mascots in *Sports Illustrated*, written about in the *Daily Gamecock* and even pictured on the sides of the *Daily Gamecock* paper boxes around Columbia. Mary and I have been in the *Lexington Woman* and *Aiken Woman* magazines and in the *Go Aiken* lifestyle magazine. My picture is in the book commemorating the back-to-back national baseball championships and, of course, I have been on *GameDay* twice.

We also have been videoed multiple times. The one Taylor Kearnes did on the love affair between Ron and Mary and the university would have brought tears to my eyes if I had tear ducts. They always say they do all this for the love of the university but I think either the love or the money is about to run out and so the (almost) final chapter of this tale…

**Figure 35: First *GameDay* (notice Ron with SBS behind podium)**

**Figure 36: SBS likes his wine on *GameDay***

**Figure 37: What a foursome!**

Figure 38: SBS has his own paper boxes in Columbia

# Sir Big Spur Day

February 5, 2014, was proclaimed Sir Big Spur Day by the South Carolina House of Representatives. Introduced by Representative Clyburn and signed unanimously by all the members of the House of Representatives, the proclamation "recognized the love and support given by Mary Snelling and Ron Albertelli to the University of South Carolina." The entire crew was present for the proclamation with our special invited guests Chase Mizell, student body president; Larry and John Friday, previous SBS marketing directors; Chris Hartley, friend; and Monica Cromer, director of development, USC College of Nursing. Again, although invited, the USC Athletic Department was not represented. During the invocation and national anthem, I got so excited that I had to join in by crowing. That was a first for the State House and brought smiles to everyone (except Mary, who was embarrassed at my rudeness). After the proclamation was read, I spent an hour having my picture taken with hundreds of people, including some Clemson fans. Below is the actual wording of the proclamation.

## A HOUSE RESOLUTION

TO PROCLAIM FEBRUARY 5, 2014, "SIR BIG SPUR DAY" IN SOUTH CAROLINA, AND TO RECOGNIZE THE LOVE AND SUPPORT GIVEN BY MARY SNELLING AND RON ALBERTELLI TO THE UNIVERSITY OF SOUTH CAROLINA.

**WHEREAS,** for the past fifteen years, Mary Snelling and Ron Albertelli have provided Sir Big Spur, the Old English Black Breasted Red Gamecock, the official live mascot and symbol of the University of South Carolina; and

**WHEREAS,** Mary Snelling and Ron Albertelli have transported Sir Big Spur at their own expense all over the United States in support of Gamecock athletics: to baseball and football regular season and championship games, as well as occasionally to other sports; and

**WHEREAS,** Sir Big Spur has been featured in news stories on national and local television networks, such as ESPN, SEC Network and Fox Sports. Sir Big Spur was also recognized by *Sports Illustrated* as one of the top five live mascots in college sports; and

**WHEREAS,** Mary Snelling and Ron Albertelli have provided Sir Big Spur purely out of their love for the University of South Carolina and for the Athletics Department, not having missed many games since 1996; and

**WHEREAS,** Sir Big Spur has brought joy to the thousands of Gamecock fans, respect to the thousands of students, and fostered a championship mentality in Gamecock athletes.

**NOW THEREFORE,**

**BE IT RESOLVED** by the House of Representatives:

**THAT** the members of the House of Representatives of the State of South Carolina, by this resolution, proclaim February 5, 2014, "Sir Big Spur Day" in South Carolina, and recognize the love and support given by Mary Snelling and Ron Albertelli to the University of South Carolina.

**BE IT FURTHER RESOLVED** that a copy of this resolution be provided to Mary Snelling and Ron Albertelli.

**Signed by the Speaker and Clerk of the House of Representatives 2-4-14**

# Epilogue: Where Do We Go from Here

So that is my story to this date. It is all the things Mary said it would be in the foreword but the ending could be all tragedy.

After multiple meetings with the athletics director and some assistant directors, with and without legal representation, and volumes of e-mails and several written "agreements," there is no agreement.

Ron and Mary have proposed several ideas for the "perpetuation of this madness," as Ron says. Those ideas have involved the Columbia Zoo; the USC equestrian center; the USC golf course; the fraternities, sororities and student service organizations of the university and the local poultry farmers. Personally I love living at Sir Big Spur's Roost and being cared for by Ron and Mary but I understand how hard they work and how they could use some help. This is the time element.

Also, Ron and Mary have expended countless thousands of dollars on equipment, equipment maintenance and travel for the past nineteen years. They own me and all trademarks associated with me and my progeny. They have proposed multiple profit sharing ideas associated with the use of me, my image and my trademarks to the university and the university has not agreed to share in any equitable manner. There was one occasion where profit sharing was tried (Sir Big Spur T-shirts); no money has been given to Mary and Ron yet. The university neglected to ask Stephen Malkoff to present his portrait at a football game (requested by Ron and Mary) as was done at Auburn, Alabama and Clemson. (I REALLY hate for the orange rednecks to outclass us.) The sale of portraits would have helped with expenses. This is the financial element.

**Figure 39: No money ever received from USC for this use of SBS's trademark**

I have become a well-recognized emblem of the University of South Carolina. The students, future students (biddies), fans, alumni and media love me and I love them. I have become a part of the University of South Carolina. I am not, as one famous lawyer once stated, "just a good idea."

Mary and Ron are ready to retire as the mascot handlers at USC. However, they are not ready to forfeit the hard work, expenses and, especially, the legacy of Sir Big Spur. They are willing to participate in a handoff to a younger or more sustainable future for SBS.

I hope my story has a happy ending.

If not, it was a great ride and we will always be yours with love,

Sir Big Spur, Mary and Ron

## About the Author

Born and raised in Aiken, South Carolina, Mary F. Snelling has been a Gamecock since birth. She received her bachelor of science in nursing and her master of science in public health from the University of South Carolina. Snelling served more than thirty years as an RN, largely with veterans affairs. Along with her husband, Ron Albertelli, she owns and cares for the family of Sir Big Spurs.

*Cock Tales* is Snelling's first book. She loves sports, music, reading, and all things Gamecock.

Contact Information

Like Sir Big Spur on Facebook.
Tweet him @spur_sir
Email him at thesirbigspur@yahoo.com
Purchase his products @ sirbigspur.com

www.ingramcontent.com/pod-product-compliance
Lightning Source LLC
Chambersburg PA
CBHW042001150426
43194CB00002B/86